Amalgamated

Amrita Dhal

BookLeaf Publishing

India | USA | UK

Presentation by *BookLeaf Publishing*

Web: www.bookleafpub.com

E-mail: info@bookleafpub.com

ISBN:9789363312463

First edition 2024

ACKNOWLEDGEMENT

I'd like to acknowledge my father and sister for always being supportive. Also, all of the people that have showered me with kind words about my writing and encouraged me to keep at it.

PREFACE

My mother's loss in 2020 changed my life and worldview. I realized how little was being said and talked about grief and how any mention of it would make the people around me uncomfortable. This experience compelled me to write my thoughts and feelings surrounding grief. It's been equal parts heartbreaking and cathartic. Someone had rightly said, "grief is all the love you have but can't give." I hope you find solace in my work and it can in some way be a cathartic experience for you too.

Grief, my forever companion

Some days I sit across from my grief and look
straight into it's eyes
I allow it to get loud, really loud I let it take me
places where I'm afraid to go, I let it show me
things I'm afraid to see
On these days, I call it by its name
I embrace it like a friend, it's someone I can trust
Every other emotion ebbs and flows
But my grief remains constant
It stays when I'm happy
It stays when I'm sad
It stays when it's bright
It stays when it's dark
It's not the companion I was looking for but it's
the companion that chose me
It's in the things I love
It's in the things I dislike

It's a reminder of what my life was like and it
could've been like
The person I used to be and a person I can no
longer be
It whispers in my ears
Everything else and everyone else will be
momentary but grief will always be by my side

Motherless daughter

Sometimes I catch my reflection in mirrors or window panes in stores and wonder can people tell I'm a motherless daughter?
Can my friends tell my smile is a little dimmer now?
Can the people I meet for the first time tell I'm a little dead on the inside?
Do my loved ones notice I tell them I love them every opportunity I get because I'm afraid there won't be a next time?
Will my children know I loved them harder because that's how I want them to remember me, exactly how I remember my mother as the most loving creature on earth?

Call me by your name

I think so often about you that your name slips
out of my mouth no matter who I'm calling out
to
But I know I don't cross your mind like that
Yet I'm the one you reach out to when you're in
need
Is it then so wrong of me to wish for you to
never not need me because it's the only way you
let me in?
But my wishes continue to remain only wishes
You live on pretending that you did nothing
wrong
And I live on pretending like I'm still strong

Love makes the world go round

If love was so common, people wouldn't write so many songs about it
If love was so common, people wouldn't get heartbroken over it
If love was so common, its presence wouldn't make people feel like they can reach for the moon
If love was so common, its absence wouldn't feel so fatal
If love was so common, the insipidity of this world wouldn't seem so glaring

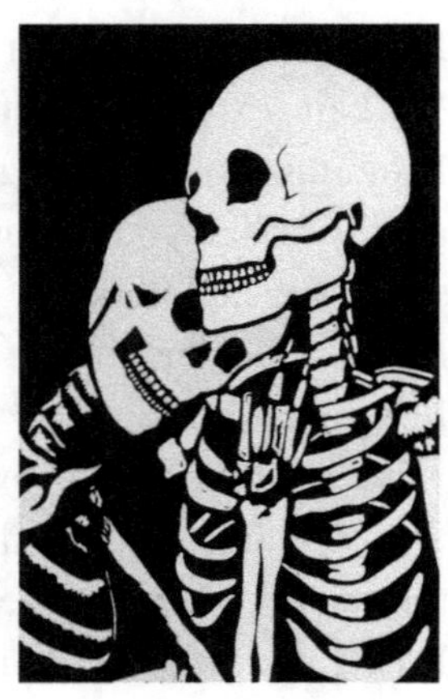

Reflection

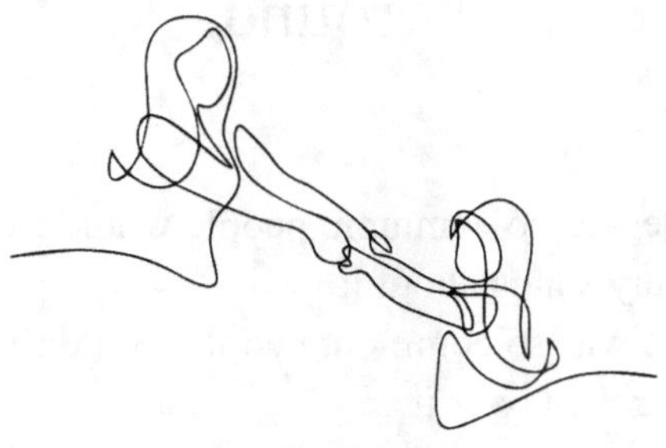

Sometimes I look at myself in the mirror and
think to myself how much I look like you
How my eyes light up when I smile exactly at
the points where yours did
How people would confuse me for you when I'd
answer your phone sometimes
It amazes me how one half of my finger nails are
like yours and the other half like papa's
My hair texture is exactly like yours to touch
I sometimes like to sing while doing mundane
activities like you did but I doubt my voice
sounds as melodious
My laugh is the loudest and fills up the room
like yours did
I like inviting friends over and cook up a storm
for them and decorate the house like you would
All the love I can't give you I make up for it by
loving people around me a little extra

I think I feel my feelings a lot more now than I
did before and most days I wish I didn't have to
lose you to feel more

Old school

I love handwritten notes and wildflowers
I love the mountains and the seas
I love the sound of your voice when you laugh
All this time I thought I had to be lost in love
when in reality I needed to be found
Loving you helped me learn how to love me

Beauty in the clichés and magic in the mundane

There's beauty in the clichés and magic in the
mundane
Send me handwritten letters and call me
old-fashioned
Gather them wildflowers and make me a
bouquet
Stay up at night so we can ogle at the million
stars
Call me names that only you and I can recall
Ugly cry until the pain washes away and silly
laugh so it makes me laugh harder
Sing me songs at the crack of dawn
Climb mountains, swim in oceans, and walk
with me in the moonlight
I need to feel alive again because I'm trying to
live for 2 you see, for my mother and me

There's beauty in the clichés and magic in the
mundane

Fantasies

I want to sit on the kitchen counter top while I
watch you cook and tell me where you learnt to
make that dish
I want to hear the story of why your mum calls
you by that nickname
I want to sip tea with you on the porch in the
evening and watch the rain pour down
I'll try to take your glasses off without waking
you because you forgot to put them aside before
you dozed off while reading
I want to slow dance in the living room on a
Sunday night while we drink our wine
I want to experience these missable moments
and turn them into unmissable memories

Resilience

I hear whispers in the hall, they call her resilient,
strong, unrelenting
Will they believe her if she said, all she did was
wake up and show up because there was no
other choice?
She reads about how you can't pour from an
empty cup but that's all she's ever done her
entire life

Love or destruction?

There isn't a waking hour when I'm not thinking
of you
I force myself to sleep to escape thoughts of you
Thoughts become images, and images turn into
dreams, and my brain creates an illusion that
you're within my reach
Reminding me of the first time I saw you; your
hair, your eyes, and your million dollar smile
You say you had no love to give but then how did I
always feel so safe in your embrace?
Your voice is a like a drug that helps me not drown
in the abyss of darkness
My mind tries to forget but the body reminds it of
all the places it's been touched
It lets a shiver down my spine, how does the body
remember?
I'd promised myself to never self-destruct in love
again, and here I am losing my mind over you

Martyrs

Here's to women
who are warriors, who've raised warriors
who are survivors, who've nurtured survivors
who loved, who've taught how to love
who grieve, who've comforted
who save, who've been saved

We're living and thriving because of every
single one of them that fought our fight before
us

For every time a woman wins, she's winning on
behalf of every woman that's lived, lives, and
will live

Little things

15

It's the little things you fall in love with, don't
you?
The smirk on their face when they're teasing
you
The twinkle in their eyes when they're talking
about their passion project
The kindness with which they talk to strangers
The softness with which they tell you a story
from their childhood
The way their nose crinkles when they're
adjusting their glasses
Something about the way they call your name

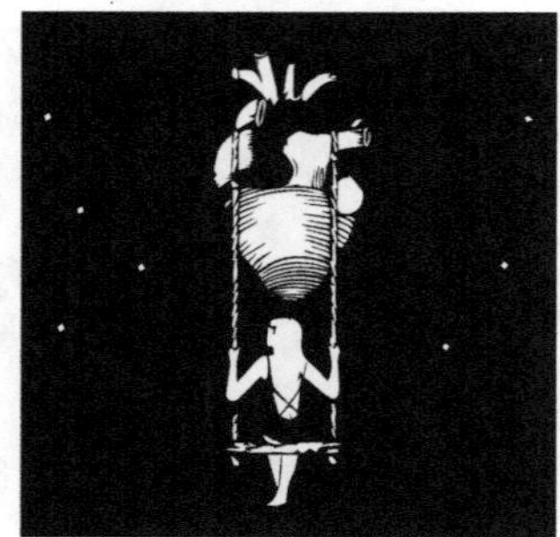

Building homes

How do people and not places feel more like
home sometimes?
How does an embrace feel safer than a room
sometimes?
How can someone's mere presence make you
more appreciative of life?
How do you then subdue your urge to shield
them from the hurt when they're sharing a story
that's caused them pain?
How would you then ever go back to living a
life that didn't feel like home again?

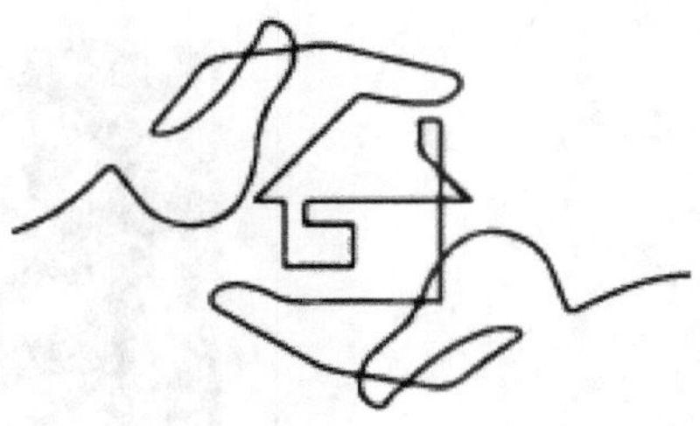

Wishful thinking

I remember dates, places, people, and faces
I like calls over texts and spring over fall
I crave for walks in the parks and sunlit paths
I look forward to days where we laugh until we
cry and hesitate to say our goodbyes
I wanna sing to the rising moon and fall asleep
at dawn, otherwise the world seems far too gone

What do you seek?

Something about the way you say my name
makes it sound so much sweeter
Is it because you say it with so much kindness?
Is it kindness that we're seeking then? And not
love?
Or maybe kindness is love?
I guess they lied to us that love stories are meant
to be great
When all that love is meant to make us feel is
happy

The skeptic

Here's to the one whose inquisitive mind is a
rare encounter in this otherwise predictable
world
Who walks around with a bag full of jokes that
spill out in moments when you didn't think you
could spare a smile, let alone laugh
Someone who is equal parts order and disorder
With an unusual appreciation for both bright
sunrises and the dark night
If the heavens could talk, they'd sing you praises
but the skeptic in you still wouldn't believe them

Regrets

I miss you and I wish I could drag you out, call
you, or text you to tell you, "Look up, the moon
looks beautiful tonight"
I take pictures of sunsets and night skies and
they're no longer being sent to you
I can only hope that you're catching a glimpse of
it too

Habitual

The weekly oiling of your hair by your mother
You think your father won't make it to the school
annual day function but you see him in the
crowd from the stage
Sharing your first alcoholic beverage with your
younger sibling
Your friend bringing you Frooti every time they
come over to your house because you told them
once how much you love it
Your crush texting you first
You reach late for a movie but they're only
showing commercials yet
Your lover bringing you flowers on your dates
Your barista remembering your coffee order
A baby clinging on to you among all the adults
they met that evening
A dog laying their head in your lap

A dish turning out exactly like the first time you
ever tasted it
You find the outfit washed and ironed that you
envisioned to wear for an impromptu event
Holding the hand of a loved one when you're
walking by a lake
Entering your house after a vacation and
sleeping in your own bed
We forget how these things made us feel once
when they happen often
I wish we could hold on to that initial feeling so
these moments never felt dimmer

Memories

The word "memory" becomes so much more
meaningful and powerful when that's the only
way you're keeping your loved one alive, in your
memories
You cling on to every tiny detail of it and replay
it in your head with immense fervor with the
hope that you'll recollect more moments that
you'd probably not paid attention to before

Pieces of me

I've collected pieces from places I lived in or
traveled to
Then there are places I've lived in or traveled to
but I didn't carry back any pieces of memorabilia
So many more places left to see and experience
and I wait eagerly to add to my tiny collection
Every place I've ever been in has stolen a piece
of my heart and replaced it with an undying
memory
I wonder if these places remember me like I
remember them?

Life lessons

Things I've learnt in the last couple of years:
Rate the doing, not the being
Humans aren't good or bad, actions are
You don't have to be enough for others, you just
have to be enough for yourself
If you're constantly anxious around certain
people, places, or events, go ahead and leave
Your anxious body is trying to be your friend
and protect you
It's okay to say no

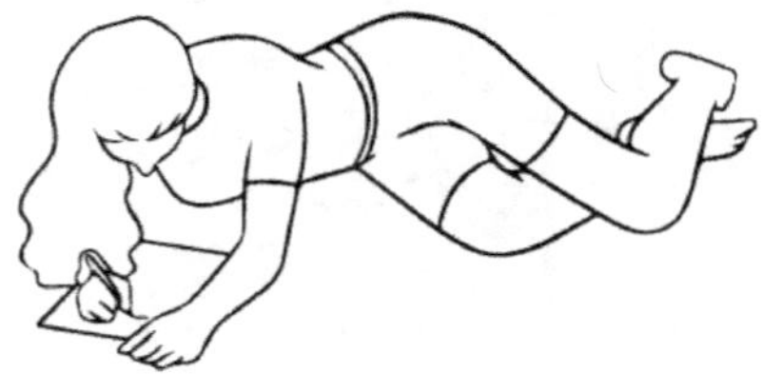

www.ingramcontent.com/pod-product-compliance
Lightning Source LLC
LaVergne TN
LVHW021339200726
843509LV00014B/2578